The Science of COMPUTERS

Clive Gifford

Crabtree Publishing Company

www.crabtreebooks.com

Crabtree Publishing Company

www.crabtreebooks.com

1-800-387-7650

Published in Canada
Crabtree Publishing
616 Welland Ave.
St. Catharines, ON
L2M 5V6

Published in the United States
Crabtree Publishing
PMB 59051, 350 Fifth Ave.
59th Floor,
New York, NY

First published in 2015 by Wayland
(A division of Hachette Children's Books)
Copyright © Wayland 2015

Author: Clive Gifford
Commissioning editor: Debbie Foy
Project editor: Caroline West (Blue Dragonfly Ltd.)
Editorial director: Kathy Middleton
Project Coordinator: Kelly Spence
Editor: Petrina Gentile
Consultant: Lee Martin, B. Ed
Designer: Mark Latter (Blue Dragonfly Ltd.)
Proofreader: Shannon Welbourn
Prepress technician: Margaret Amy Salter
Print and production coordinator: Margaret Amy Salter

Printed in Canada/022015/MA20150101

Photographs:
All images courtesy of Shutterstock except: p6
Bletchley Park Trust/Science & Society Picture
Library; p7 (bottom right) Science Museum/
Science & Society Picture Library; and p29
(centre right) IStockphoto/Staffan Andersson.

While every attempt has been made to clear
copyright, should there be any inadvertent
omission this will be rectified in future editions.

Disclaimer: The website addresses (URLs)
included in this book were valid at the time
of going to press. However, because of the
nature of the Internet, it is possible that some
addresses may have changed, or sites may have
changed or closed down since publication.
While the author and publisher regret any
inconvenience this may cause the readers, no
responsibility for any such changes can be
accepted by either the author or the publisher.
Note to reader: Words highlighted in bold
appear in the Glossary on page 30.
Answers to activities are on page 31.

Library and Archives Canada Cataloguing in Publication

Gifford, Clive, author
    The science of computers / Clive Gifford.

(Get connected to digital literacy)
Includes index.
Issued in print and electronic formats.
ISBN 978-0-7787-1510-8 (bound).--ISBN 978-0-7787-1562-7
(pbk.).--
ISBN 978-1-4271-1587-4 (pdf).--ISBN 978-1-4271-1583-6 (html)

    1. Computers--Juvenile literature. 2. Information
technology--
Juvenile literature. I. Title.

TK7885.5.G53 2015   j004   C2014-908285-1
                                         C2014-908286-X

Library of Congress Cataloging-in-Publication Data

Gifford, Clive, author.
The science of computers / Clive Gifford.
    pages cm. -- (Get connected to digital literacy)
Includes index.
 ISBN 978-0-7787-1510-8 (reinforced library binding : alk. paper)
-- ISBN 978-0-7787-1562-7 (pbk. : alk. paper) --
ISBN 978-1-4271-1587-4 (electronic pdf : alk. paper) --
ISBN 978-1-4271-1583-6 (electronic html : alk. paper)
1. Computer science--Juvenile literature. 2. Computers--Juvenile
literature. I. Title.

QA76.23.G54 2015
004--dc23
                              2014047274

Contents

A World of Computers

Computers are amazing machines. They are able to store, handle, and retrieve information, which is known as data. Computers can be programmed in different ways to perform a huge variety of tasks.

Computers everywhere

Computer technology is found in the unlikeliest of places. Things that you don't think of as computers, such as microwave ovens, toasters, cameras, and traffic lights, all have computer technology inside them and are **programmed** to perform a limited set of tasks. Other computers, such as laptops or tablets, can do lots of different jobs.

Desktop computers

Also known as PCs, these have a case and usually a separate screen. PCs are found in millions of homes, schools, and offices.

Laptops

Also known as notebooks, these are portable computers with a battery inside for working away from home. Almost all laptops feature a solid keyboard for typing.

In-car computers

These constantly check on the car's engine and other important parts. They can often adjust how the car performs, as well as warn drivers when there is a problem.

Washing machines

Did you know that the different cycles of wash performed by a washing machine are controlled by a small computer?

Tablets

Slim, lightweight, and battery-powered, these devices have a screen that you touch and swipe to read books, watch videos, play games, and many other things.

ATM machines

Bank machines dispense cash when someone inserts a card. They are linked to computers inside the bank that keep track of the money.

Smartphones

These cell phones have real computing power inside their small cases. For example, you can check emails, view websites, and play music.

TRUE STORY

Pump Up The Power Computers are getting faster and more powerful. For example, the latest Xbox One games console has more power than the flight computer that controlled the United States Space Shuttles on their 135 missions into space.

Games consoles

These are packed with computing power to run amazing, action packed games.

The Incredible Shrinking Computer

The first programmable computers were developed in the 1940s. Many were huge machines that filled whole rooms, but computer parts soon got smaller, faster, and more reliable.

This picture shows the control panels of the Colossus Mark II from 1943, which was the world's first programmable computer.

⬇ Early computers

Early computers used hundreds or thousands of large electrical parts to act as switches and to store information. They often broke down.

Electronic Numerical Integrator And Computer, or ENIAC, was an early computer used in the United States from 1946 to 1955. In ten years, the longest period it worked without needing to replace a part was just five days.

ENIAC was almost the size of a basketball court. In 1995, 40 years after it was switched off, computing students managed to put all of ENIAC's functions on a single **silicon chip** that measured 7.5mm by 5.3mm–which is smaller than your fingernail.

The smallest silicon chips contain thousands of tiny circuits.

A Real Heavyweight The Sage computer was designed in the 1950s to track enemy aircraft. It was the world's heaviest computer system, weighing 227 tons, which is as much as 38 adult elephants!

Some silicon chips are so small that ants can carry them.

Shrinking chips!

From the late 1950s and onwards, engineers shrank the size of a computer's parts so lots of them could fit on a tiny wafer of material. This integrated **circuit**, or silicon chip, could also be built cheaper than traditional parts. Silicon chips also worked faster and were more reliable.

COMPUTER Hero!

Charles Babbage tried to build the first computers in the 1820s and 1830s out of metal gears and other parts. Babbage didn't complete his "engines," but was a pioneer, building many parts that would be needed in modern computers.

Charles Babbage

Here's the Hardware

Steve Wozniak

The parts of a computer you can touch, such as the case, screen, and insides, are called its hardware. But a computer with just hardware won't do a thing. It also needs the programs stored inside.

Steve Wozniak built the first Apple personal computer. His business partner, Steve Jobs, sold his camper van to help raise money to buy the parts. The pair made 100 computers in 10 days in 1976 and sold them for around $580 each.

⬇ Operating systems

The collection of programs, or software that controls how a computer works is called an **operating system**, or OS. Android, for example, is a popular operating system for smartphones and tablets. Other programs work with the operating system to let you send emails, play games, or do your homework.

The Android robot

⬇ Plugged in

Extra pieces of hardware called **peripherals** can be attached to most computers. You can physically attach some of these using a cable. Other peripherals are wireless and work with the computer by sending and receiving signals carried by light or radio waves.

PC PORTS

The back of a PC has lots of sockets, called ports, that let you plug in different peripherals. You can see some of the most common ports here.

This picture shows the back of a computer without the plastic casing that surrounds the different ports.

1. Monitor
This port connects a monitor screen to a computer to display programs or images.

2. USB
Universal Serial Bus, or USB ports, accept a range of different peripherals such as a USB mouse (see page 17) and a printer (see page 20).

3. Ethernet Port
This port takes a cable that connects a PC to a network of other computers.

4. Audio
Speakers and headphones are plugged into these ports to play sounds from the computer.

STRETCH YOURSELF

Find the Computer Port
Here are images of three different ports.

Can you figure out what each port is used for by answering the following questions:

☞ Which port connects a USB mouse to a computer?

☞ Which port connects headphones to a computer?

☞ Which port is used for plugging in monitors?

a

b

c

Answers on page 31

Let's Look Inside

If you open up the desktop or tower case of a typical PC and peek inside, you'll find that nearly all computers have lots of similar parts.

CD/DVD drive
This box plays compact discs and DVDs on the computer or is used to load programs onto the machine.

PSU
A power supply unit, or PSU, takes electricity from an outlet and supplies it to the rest of the computer.

Hard disk
This stores large amounts of data and programs (see page 14). Tablets and some laptops use memory chips instead of hard disks for storage.

Fan
A computer's parts can get hot, so a fan inside blows cooling air over them.

Cards
These cards are printed circuit boards that have electronic parts fitted to them to do a particular job. A sound card, for example, will generate and play all the sounds a computer can make.

Expansion slots
These are spare places for slotting extra cards into the computer.

MOTHERBOARD

A **motherboard** is a circuit board that contains connections to other parts of the computer. It features crucial parts such as two types of computer memory, **RAM** and **ROM**, and the **CPU**–which is the real brains of the computer.

2. ROM
(Read Only Memory)
This cannot be changed by a user, but stores programs and information even when the computer is switched off. ROM also holds the instructions that are used to start a computer.

1. CPU
(Central Processing Unit)
This is a powerful chip known as a microprocessor. The CPU does all the computer's calculations and also controls its other parts.

3. RAM
(Random Access Memory)
A computer uses silicon chips containing RAM as its temporary workspace for storing programs and data while it is working. RAM chips connect to the motherboard using these memory slots. When you turn off a computer, the RAM empties and the data is lost.

TRUE STORY

Let's Cool Off When working hard, some CPUs get hotter than the boiling point of water, which is 212°F (100°C).
A fan and **heat sink** carries heat away from the CPU to cool them down.

STAY SAFE!

Computers are powered by electricity, which can harm you if you are not careful. Follow these tips to stay safe:

1. Always unplug a computer before you move it.

2. Never yank a plug out of its socket by the wire. Pull it out gently holding the plastic casing.

3. Only ever hold the casing of a plug when you plug it into, or take it out of, a socket. Never touch the pins.

4. Never let water or any liquid get close to a computer.

Data and Circuits

Computers are useful because they can handle lots of information. They do this by breaking down the information into numbers that their electrical circuits can process quickly.

Ins and outs

All computers receive data from a source, known as an input. They interact with the data based on their programs, which is called processing. They then output the results of the processing in different ways, such as displaying numbers on a screen or sending commands to a robot that the computer is controlling.

Input ⟩⟩ Processing ⟩⟩ Output

Storage

COMPUTER BRAIN

You perform just like a computer when you are given a math equation to do. The input is hearing or reading the problem, the processing is adding up the numbers, and the output is saying the answer or writing it down.

Electric numbers

Computers store and process all sorts of data, such as photographs and music, as long streams of **binary** numbers, which use only two digits: 0 and 1. A computer's chips are packed with electrical circuits and switches. The data flows around these circuits as patterns of tiny pulses of electrical signals, which represent the ones and zeros.

 # STRETCH YOURSELF

Build an Electrical Circuit
You can see how electricity flows through a circuit by making a simple electrical circuit and switch. Ask an adult to help you connect up a battery, a small light bulb, some electrical wire, a small piece of wood, two thumbtacks, and a paper clip in the same way as the diagram below.

Why is the paper clip so important?
The paper clip is the circuit switch. When you put it on the thumbtacks, the circuit is completed. Electricity flows from the battery around the whole circuit and lights up the bulb. Removing the paper clip breaks the circuit and switches off the bulb.

Small light bulb

Electrical wire

Battery

Paper clip

Thumbtacks

Small piece of wood

Memory Matters

Computers use other types of memory besides the RAM and ROM found on their motherboards. These all play a role in storing programs or information.

Do You Remember?

RAM
Random Access Memory

ROM
Read-Only Memory

(see page 11)

Byte size

Memory is measured in bytes—lots of them. In a single **byte**, there are usually eight binary digits. A kilobyte is 1,024 bytes, but computers today work in megabytes and gigabytes. Each one of the following measures of memory is approximately 1,000 times bigger than the last.

Spinning disks

Hard disks are found in many computers and also in digital recorders that record TV programs. Hard disks can store hundreds of gigabytes on their spinning metal platters. In some hard disks, these platters spin around as fast as 200 times a second!

KB Kilobyte	MB Megabyte	GB Gigabyte	TB Terabyte
1,000 bytes	1,000,000 bytes	1,000,000,000 bytes	1,000,000,000,000 bytes

A single gigabyte or GB of memory can hold over 8 billion binary numbers—that's more figures than the number of people on the planet! Many smartphones come with a built-in memory of 16GB or more.

Add more memory

You can easily increase a computer's storage abilities by plugging in external memory. This might be a memory card, which can be the size of a postage stamp or even smaller, or an external hard disk in its own case.

Another form of external memory is a flash drive. This plugs into a USB port and contains a small memory chip.

Back it up

Good computer users always make a regular backup or copy of their files. You can store this backup on a flash drive, an external hard disk, or a CD. If there's a problem with your computer, then all your important files will still be safe and secure.

TRUE STORY

Heavy Hard Disk The first hard disk was built in 1956. The huge IBM 350 disk storage unit weighed almost 1,000 kg (1 ton) and could only be moved by a forklift truck. It held just 3.75 megabytes, which is a tiny fraction of the memory in today's cell phones.

STRETCH YOURSELF

Sorting Data

Ask an adult to help you work out the size of some typical files on a computer using a computer's file manager program.

Write down the size of files holding a movie video, a music file, and a document, such as a letter.

 Which was the biggest?

 Can you use a calculator to work out how many of each type of file would fit on the different memory devices below?

Memory card 2,000MB

CD-Rom 650MB

Hard disk drive (HDD) 100,000MB

Input Devices: Keyboards, Mice, and Trackpads

All computers need ways for you to enter commands or data. There are many different types of input devices. The ones people use most often are a keyboard, mouse, and trackpad.

Computer keyboards

A keyboard lets you type words and numbers into a computer to write an email or control a program. Each key is a switch. When you press a key down, it sends a signal to the computer to let it know it has been pressed.

A row of function keys (F1 to F12) calls up different options depending on the program you're using. Pressing F1 in many programs, for example, opens help information.

You press the arrow or cursor keys to move around the screen.

Some keyboards are made out of flexible plastic and can be rolled up and packed away.

This virtual keyboard is made of a grid of light beams projected onto a flat surface. You type by letting your fingers touch the light making up each key.

Computer mice

A mouse is a handy tool that lets you move a pointer, called a **cursor**, around the screen. Buttons on the mouse let you select options in a program. There is often a scroll wheel in between the buttons. You can use this to scroll or move up or down the screen to look through a long document.

COMPUTER Hero!

Douglas Engelbart was an American computer engineer. In 1963, he built the first mouse out of wood with a single red button. Engelbart's mouse didn't catch on for 20 years, but since then over one billion have been sold.

Trackpads

Found on laptops, these flat pads use your finger to control the cursor on screen. A grid of electrical circuits underneath the pad detects the movement and turns it into electrical signals that are then sent back to the computer.

You can also get separate trackpads that work in the same way as integrated ones, but are designed for desktop computers rather than laptops.

More Input Devices: Touch Screens and Scanners

You don't always need a keyboard or mouse to send data or commands to a computer. Some computers and smartphones, for example, react to your voice or the touch of a screen.

Touchy feely screens

Tablets, many phones, and some laptops have a touch screen. When you press the screen or move your fingers across it, the device will perform different tasks, depending on the program you are using. For example, swiping the screen while reading an **eBook** can make the page turn, just like a real book.

Pinch and zoom

Some multi-touch screens recognize two touches at the same time. When two fingers touch the screen and move outwards, the computer zooms in on part of the screen to give you a close-up view. Moving your fingers together, which is called a pinch, does the opposite.

Scan that

Document scanners turn the writing and images on a piece of paper into data that a computer can store and use. Scanners are often used in offices, but you can also use them at home to copy documents or photos.

Barcode scanners

A barcode is a pattern of black and white stripes on items you buy in stores. At the checkout, a special scanner can recognize an item from its code, compare this to the shop's database of items, and call up the price.

Graphics tablets

A graphics tablet is like a larger, but more accurate, trackpad (see page 17), but you use a pen-shaped **stylus** instead of your fingertips. Designers, fashion designers, and artists, as well as cartoon and movie animators, use graphics tablets. They can select different colors, brush sizes, and other effects. Graphics tablets are also used by architects to design buildings.

Output Devices

After running programs and processing data, a computer passes on the results of its work. This is called its output. Computer screens, printers, and loudspeakers are all types of output devices.

Print it out

A printer turns the computer's output into a hard copy on paper for you to read and keep. **Inkjet** printers, for example, allow people to print digital photos and documents from a computer in colour.

STRETCH YOURSELF

Print a Greeting Card

Ask an adult to help you design and print out a greeting card. Whatever computer and program you are using, set the paper to landscape, which means the paper is wider than it is taller.

Put the main picture on the right half of the page, so that when you print it out you can fold the paper in half and finish the card.

STRETCH YOURSELF

Can You Help Save the Planet?

Millions of plastic inkjet cartridges are sold worldwide each year. Most are thrown away when they are empty, but can take a long time to break down in the environment.

Your task is to find out some different ways to recycle these cartridges. Why not also ask your teacher to help you set up a cartridge-recycling box at school?

3D printing

Some printers can print actual objects. A three-dimensional or 3D design of the object is created on a computer. The design is then sent as a file to a 3D printer. This "prints" a thin layer of the object using a material such as plastic or metal instead of ink. It continues on printing in layers until the whole object is complete.

The range of objects that have already been 3D-printed is amazing—from car parts and sculptures to smartphone cases and jewelry. Scientists are even working on how to print replacement teeth and other body parts!

This flying robot drone is controlled by a computer program. The commands sent to the drone are the computer's output.

Your wish is my command

Robots and remote-controlled machines are also output devices controlled by a computer. Robots are used in factories, for example, to do jobs usually performed by humans. An example of a remote-controlled machine is an unmanned aerial vehicle or UAV, which is an airplane that can fly without a pilot.

Sounds Amazing

Early computers were silent or only made beeping noises. Today's computers can be noisy machines, playing music, and blasting out sound effects from games.

Computer sound

Sounds are caused by vibrations that travel through the air as waves. These sound waves can be gathered by a microphone, which turns them into electrical signals. A **sound card** or sound processing chip inside a computer can convert these electrical signals into computer data by turning lots of little samples of the sound into numbers. This data is stored as a **sound file**.

Sound shaping

Once stored on a computer, the sounds can be replayed or they can be edited and changed using computer programs. Sound files can also be transferred between computers or loaded into the memory of a portable music player or a smartphone.

When a sound file is played, it is turned back into electrical signals that are sent to a loudspeaker. These signals make the cone of the loudspeaker move back and forth, moving the air to create sound waves.

A smartphone or music player may play sounds quietly. You can place them in a dock with bigger speakers and an electronic device called an amplifier to increase the loudness of the sound.

Make Some Noise!

Here are three challenges involving sound. See how many of them you can complete!

1. Sounds on the Move

A cell phone contains a microphone and most also have a sound recording program. Record some sounds on a phone while you are out and then play them back when you get home.

tinyurl.com/chngsound

2. Sing High, Sing Low

See how sounds can change note from high to low using a computer connected to the Internet. Ask an adult to help you type the address on the left into a browser and have some fun playing with sound.

3. Sounds Like Fun

Use a computer connected to the Internet to learn more about sound by visiting this web page full of different experiments and activities.

tinyurl.com/learnsounds

TRUE STORY

Mega Memories Some music players have enough memory to store 40,000 songs. That's enough to play a new song a day for 109 years!

Picture Perfect

Cameras used to store images on film. You could not see the pictures until they were developed with chemicals and printed out as photographs. Today, digital cameras display pictures on screen in an instant.

Digital cameras

Digital cameras use a special chip that turns light collected by the camera's lens into electrical signals. The camera processes the electrical signals into computer data so that your picture can be stored as an **image file.** You can then look at the picture on screen, print it out, or send it to another computer. The amount of detail a digital camera can capture is called **resolution**, which is measured in megapixels or millions of **pixels**.

TRUE STORY

Snap Happy Today, people take millions of photographs using digital cameras or cameras built into cell phones or tablets. Around 350 million digital photos are added to the social network site Facebook every day. That's an awful lot of photos!

Have some fun taking a "selfie" on a smartphone.

STRETCH YOURSELF

Shrink Your Friend

Use a digital camera or smartphone camera with two friends to take a fun optical illusion image.

Get one friend to stand a few feet away and stick out a hand. Get the other friend to stand in the distance. Line them up so it looks as if a small person is standing on the hand. You will probably need to try this a few times to get it right.

What other optical illusion images can you take?

Digital video

Videos are just a series of individual pictures taken really quickly one after another. When played back, they show a moving scene. Small, tough digital video cameras can be mounted on a sport bike or skateboarding helmet to take amazing action videos.

COMPUTER Hero!

Steve Sasson built the first digital camera in 1975. It weighed over 8 lbs (3.6 kg) and took 23 seconds to store one tiny black-and-white photograph on a cassette tape. Each picture had a resolution of just 0.01 megapixels. Today's cameras offer 1,000 times greater resolution.

Computer Gaming

Many gaming joysticks have "hot" buttons that you can program to do certain jobs in different games.

Hundreds of millions of computer games are sold every year. Some games are played on smartphones and tablets. Others are played on laptops or special gaming computers called consoles.

Game controls

Some games use the computer's keyboard, mouse, or touch screen to provide the playing controls. Other games, particularly action games, need special controllers. These controllers, or input devices might be a joystick or game pad, and let users change direction quickly in the game.

Some gamers use controllers such as this racing car steering wheel which mimics the controls of a real car.

Kinect Xbox 360

Motion sensing

Computer games using motion controllers let players make realistic movements such as swinging a racquet in a tennis game. Most motion controllers are handheld. As the player moves the motion controller around in the air, the game copies the movements and commands on the screen.

Kinect for the Xbox 360 games console does away with hand controllers. Instead, sensors detect the player's body movements as they jump or aim a kick, for example. The console then converts these into realistic movements in the game.

Mario, the hero of Super Mario Bros.

COMPUTER Hero!

Shigeru Miyamoto thought about being a manga comic artist before becoming a games designer at Nintendo. He developed Super Mario Bros., the Legend of Zelda, and other smash hits. He also helped develop Wii Fit and Wii Sports—the best-selling console game of all time.

TRUE STORY

Minecraft Madness In 2014, the government of Denmark recreated its entire country in the computer game Minecraft to get kids interested in the nation and its geography.

MEGA and Mini Machines

Some computers are faster than others. The fastest and most powerful are called supercomputers. These giant machines have thousands of processors all working together. Other computers can be as tiny as a stamp.

Supercomputers

Supercomputers are often used to make a **simulation** of complicated things, such as weather patterns, to work out what will happen next. One of the largest supercomputers, the Titan supercomputer, is kept in 200 large cabinets. It works thousands of times faster than a desktop computer. In 2013, the Tianhe-2 supercomputer became the fastest computer in the world. It can make 33 quadrillion calculations per second!

An example of a supercomputer

Mini computers

There are also small hobby computers such as the Raspberry Pi. This has a processor, memory, and USB ports so that you can connect it to a keyboard and screen. The Raspberry Pi is only the size of a credit card, but Intel's Edison computer is even smaller. It is only the size of a postage stamp and will one day power wearable computers in clothes.

COMPUTER Hero!

American computer engineer **Seymour Cray** is regarded as the father of supercomputers. His first computer, the CDC 6600 in 1963, could make 9 million calculations every second. His 1976 Cray-1 supercomputer was 20 times faster. Both were the fastest computers in the world at the time of their launch.

The Raspberry Pi is often used in schools for fun learning activities. You can also program it to play games and control robots.

Cray-1

STRETCH YOURSELF

Design a Wearable Computer

Can you figure out how to design your own wearable computer?

Here are some questions to ask yourself:

☞ How will it be powered?

☞ Where will you put the display?

☞ How would the user control the computer?

☞ What is its use or purpose?

Glossary

binary A number system containing only zeros and ones

byte A small unit of memory that can hold up to eight binary digits

circuit A path along which an electric signal can be carried

Central Processing Unit (CPU) A powerful series of electronic circuits that perform all the calculations in a computer and also control the machine's other parts

cursor A moving symbol, such as an arrow or flashing block, which shows a position on a computer's screen

eBook A type of computer file containing all the text and images of a book, which is accessible by a computer

heat sink A device that cools some types of silicon chip by carrying heat away from them

image file A type of computer file that holds a photograph or illustration

inkjet A type of printer that uses ink forced out of tiny holes, called jets, to print

motherboard A printed electrical circuit board containing key parts of a computer and with connections for other circuit boards to join

operating system The computer programs that run a computer's basic functions and manage other programs running on the system

peripherals Devices such as printers, mice, or keyboards that connect to a computer

pixel Short for picture element, a pixel is a single point or dot, thousands or millions of which make up a digital image or a computer display such as a touch screen

programmed When a computer is given a set of instructions so that it works in a particular way

Random Access Memory (RAM) A type of computer memory that can store information and be rewritten

resolution The amount of detail that a digital camera can capture or a monitor screen can display. It is measured in megapixels or millions of pixels

Read Only Memory (ROM) A type of permanent memory that doesn't lose data when the computer is switched off

silicon chip An integrated circuit made up of thousands or millions of microscopic electronic parts etched onto a small wafer of silicon material

simulation A computer program that acts as a model of a real-life event or system, such as a car crash or flying an aircraft

sound card A set of circuits that enables a computer to produce sounds and often to record and change them as well

sound file A type of computer file containing music, speech, or other sounds which can be played on a device such as a tablet or iPod

stylus A pencil-like object used as an input device on laptops and tablets that have touch screens

Further Resources

Books

Technology Timelines: Digital Technology by Tom Jackson (Franklin Watts, 2015)

How Does a Touch Screen Work? by Leon Gray (Gareth Stevens, 2014)

The True Cost of Technology by Mary Colson (Crabtree, 2014)

How Things Work: Electrical Gadgets by Ade Deane-Pratt (PowerKids Press, 2011)

Websites

www.computersciencelab.com/ComputerHistory/History.htm
A history of computing website with lots of pictures of exhibits.

www.explainthatstuff.com/how-computer-memory-works.html
A detailed explanation of how computer memory works written in clear English.

scitech.web.cern.ch/scitech/TopTech/03/Chip/chip2.shtml
This web page explains how silicon chips are made.

Answers

page 9 Find the Computer Port

b A port for connecting a USB mouse to a computer

c An outlet for connecting headphones to a computer

a A port for plugging in a monitor